Isn't That Pyramid Selling?

by

Ron G Holland

A VERY POSITIVE BOOK ABOUT NETWORK MARKETING!

Ron G Holland

Top Biz Guru, Author of international bestsellers Talk & Grow Rich and Turbo Success

www.RonGHolland.com

© 2009 | Ron G Holland

Second Edition - 2012

Personal Invitation from Ron G Holland to a Global Business Opportunity

Dear reader,

After 40 years of creating businesses and taking existing businesses to the next level, including big network marketing companies, I have come across a very special business opportunity to which I would like to invite you personally. I would love you to join my team and take advantage of this lucrative global SILVER AND GOLD COINS BUSINESS that literally anyone can do. This is the lowest risk and the lowest outlay business opportunity I have seen in years, and it's actually something that works for everyone.

Simply follow the link and leave your details, and I will personally contact you very quickly to show you how you can build and protect your wealth while helping others do the same. Type the link below into your web browser:

www.ISNCoins.com/RonAtWealth

Onwards and Upwards

Ron G Holland

Table of Contents:

1. What exactly is Pyramid selling? — 12
2. So what's Network Marketing? — 14
3. Network Marketing vs. Pyramid Selling - how to tell the good from the fake! — 16
4. Network Marketing - the business opportunity of the Millennium — 18
5. Remuneration and Rewards — 20
6. Working out the Best Plan for You — 25
7. Dreams, Goals, Aspirations.... … and a Desire to Make Money — 27
8. Thousands are quietly making a small fortune — 30

9.	Word of mouth advertising	32
10.	What do big corporations, governments, the military and religious organisations have in common?	34
11.	Why is network marketing so powerful?	35
12.	A Business of your Own, but not on Your Own	38
13.	Rules, Regulations and Fair Trading	39
14.	How to tell a genuine opportunity from a fake one	40
15.	What next?	43
16.	Appendix 1	43
17.	Appendix 2	47
18.	Appendix 3	50

Personal Invitation from Ron
G Holland to a Global
Business Opportunity   62

1. What exactly is Pyramid selling?

Pyramid selling is illegal. It is based on the concept that someone buys product (or service, i.e. a club membership) at a price, adds a profit margin and sells to the next person. The second person adds yet another profit margin and sells to a third person and so on, until the product becomes too expensive to sell and it ends up in someone's garage. Many times there is not even a product involved, the scheme simply revolves around people passing money to each other (a money-go-round) and relies totally on more and more people entering the scheme. So in reality, this scheme is NOT workable. Here's why. E.g: The type of product is irrelevant but for the sake of this example let's look at 1000 tins of aerosol paint which have a usual retail price of £1. These would be sold to the first "level" for, say 50p. The first level purchaser is then required to find someone else to buy the consignment for, say 60p or even 70p. Clearly after one or two trading manoeuvres the product becomes too expensive to buy in a consignment - no one will buy 1000 cans at £1 when they can buy them individually at the local shop. At each level, part of the profit is passed upwards to the level above until "the last man in the chain" gets stuck with product he cannot sell and he loses his money. This loss of money by the "last man" is inevitable from the commencement of the scheme, and as such, the system is easily identifiable as a "con" trick.

2. So what's Network Marketing?

Network Marketing (sometimes called a trading scheme, Multi-level marketing (MLM) or referral marketing) is totally different. In this case no-one ends up with a quantity of useless product in their basement or garage. Everyone buys product from the company that they use personally as well as sell to others. What's more, they only buy the amount of product that they can use/sell in a reasonable period and often only when they have a customer to buy it. They then replace their stock, as and when they need it. Following the example above, where aerosol cans of paint are the product, the following Network Marketing scenario is totally different.EG. The first difference would be the number of cans bought. Usually there is no minimum. Each can has a pre-set wholesale price, say 70p, and a recommended retail price say £1. Any member participating in the Network Marketing business can buy as much or as little stock as he/she needs at wholesale price. The idea then is to sell it at retail price and make a profit. Another major difference is that most participants usually find their customers before placing their order for product from the company. The final difference is that in network marketing most companies also operate a stock buy-back policy in the event that any participant wants to leave the scheme.

3. Network Marketing vs. Pyramid Selling - how to tell the good from the fake!

There are lots of genuine opportunities, and in turn a lot of Ponzi schemes that are well disguised under the veil of legitimateness. These are the main and simplest tell tales:

Network Marketing:

1. Minimal investment required.
2. Legal buy back arrangements.
3. No income generated from enrolments.
4. Self-promotion is a major plus.
5. Fixed buying & selling prices.

Pyramid Selling:

1. A large investment is usually needed to 'join'.
2. Distributors can be caught with large amounts of unwanted stock.
3. Major income is generated from enrolments.
4. Self-promotion is virtually non-existent.
5. Prices are set according to your position in the chain.

4. Network Marketing - the business opportunity of the Millennium

Network Marketing is a highly ethical and practical business that is currently responsible for creating sales well in excess of $16 billion dollars annually. Successful companies have a product or a service (or both) that is sold outside the network. In many instances companies follow the U.S. legal guidelines, which require over 70% of the product to be sold, or personally consumed, before more products can be purchased. This is good business practice. Furthermore, no-one in the network earns any money at all, unless product is sold. Once product is sold, however, the profit on that product is distributed to the Networkers according to the marketing plan. Networking is predominately a "people" industry in which distributors of products can earn impressive rewards for recruiting, teaching, training and motivating others to sell products and become successful.

5. Remuneration and Rewards

There are many different ways of making money in Network Marketing (network reward plans). Here are the six most common.

Unilevel

A simple plan, with unlimited width, so that the frontline can have as many people enrolled in it as you like, and a limited depth. Most Unilevel plans pay out to a depth of five levels but seven and eight are not uncommon. Many have compression to help address the limited depth pay-out.

Stair Step-Breakaway

This is presently the most common compensation plan. The plan has two sides, the front ("stair-step") and the back (breakaway"). The front side has increasing rank positions that are achieved by meeting specified volume requirements in your group until your personal volume is at a level where you and your group breakaway. Usually breakaway plans allow unlimited width, i.e. you can sponsor as many people as you like on your front line. Many of these plans have quotas and group volume requirements in order to qualify for bonuses. Most pay six levels deep, but they have been known to pay nine levels deep. Most compress volume up, so that non-active distributors don't get commission and the active ones will pick up the rewards. Override commissions are based on both personal volume and personal group sales.

Matrix

With a fixed matrix you can usually sponsor only a fixed number of people on your front line. If you sponsor more, - and you are actively encouraged to do so - then those extra distributors "spill over" into the levels below, so downlines grow much faster. Usually matrix is six wide and six deep, or two wide and twelve deep. This type of plan lends itself admirably to certain service-related products like buying and service companies and subscription sales with a fixed monthly cost. An unfixed matrix (such as the Unilevel or stair step breakaway) will allow you to sponsor unlimited people on your front line. It is important that commission payments are based on downline sales and not on filling in all the places in the matrix. It has been argued that "spill-over" can interfere with a participant's management and training responsibilities.

Binary

These plans are becoming increasingly popular. A binary plan is a fixed matrix with two wide on the front line. There are many ways in which binary plans operate, however; most of the binary plans coming out of the USA have no limit on levels and distributors are paid on the volume in the group, usually weekly. To make the most money you have to balance the two legs or sides in your organisation. If not, you will be paid out on the weak leg and the surplus money you are due on the strong leg will be held in "escrow" until you do manage to balance the legs. Participants may have business centres or income centres, rather than one fixed position in the network, and many hold a number of positions in their downlines.

Hybrid

This plan is simply a combination of other plans, i.e. they take various components from a number of plans in an endeavour to create an even more effective marketing programme. Hybrid plans started in the United States when a number of party plan operators found it beneficial to motivate their party planners to recruit as well as sell. This may not be a bad way to go, bearing in mind all plans have their "pros "and "cons." but it can become complex and hence difficult to explain toparticipants.6. Two-up The two up plan works by you giving your first two recruits to your upline sponsor. After that, the first two recruits they sponsor go to you and at that point you start earning commission. Lots of these plans have started, then failed. In fact, right now I cannot think of a single one that has succeeded. They also generally have a bad reputation.

6. Working out the Best Plan for You

All plans have their pros and cons. So, by all means look at the marketing plan, but also look beyond. Look at the products and services, the people who are already involved, the marketing literature, the Code of Ethics, the atmosphere at Business Opportunity Meetings, the training that is available, the sales and marketing tools supplied by the company.

The advantages of Network Marketing

- A business of your own
- Virtually no overheads
- Flexible working hours
- Extensive travel - often global
- A chance to build a business to any size you desire maybe even bigger than the person who introduced you to the opportunity
- A real chance of financial independence
- Time with your family - they can work and travel with you
- You are building a business of your own, but not on your own

7. Dreams, Goals, Aspirations....
... and a Desire to
... Make Money

Most people have dreams, goals, aspirations and a burning desire to make money. What they don't have is a vehicle. They don't have a product or service, a marketing method that works, or a reward system. Network marketing offers all of these and much more. Indeed, for many people it's the perfect business opportunity. For several reasons. It has a low level entry fee, it's low risk, you work when and where you want to, it's an exciting "people" business, with travel, new friends and associates and -once you've built a network - an extremely healthy cash flow. Indeed, networking offers everyone the chance to earn a very serious income, maybe a fortune, if they work hard and motivate their group to do the same. What's more, network marketing offers the same opportunity to everybody.

> *"Twenty years from now you will be more disappointed by the things that you didn't do than by the ones you did do. So throw off the bowlines. Sail away from safe harbour. Catch the trade winds in your sail. Explore. Dream. Discover."*
>
> *Mark Twain*

Whereas once Network Marketing was heavily biased towards housewives and those between jobs, today it is recognised as one of the key areas of growth for the new millennium. This fact alone has changed the demographics of network marketing beyond recognition. Already there are literally tens of thousands of professionals involved in network marketing. Doctors, lawyers, accountants, dentists, real estate people, actors, brokers, teachers, insurance salesmen. All quietly building networks and making money, in addition to their already substantial salaries. They see Network Marketing as the key to their future security and happily, while they're building their network nest-egg, the flexible working hours fit in seamlessly with their already hectic schedules.

8. Thousands are quietly making a small fortune

Network Marketing is predominantly a word-of-mouth business with people talking to each other and "sharing" their products and services. Most Networkers never need to advertise to sell their products or services, they just network! One US-based Network company alone turns over $7 billion a year and has been trading successfully for over forty years. That company advertises a little, but most don't. In fact, networking is the world's best kept secret, with millions of people all quietly beavering away on their way to a potential fortune. Some, of course, only earn an extra £50 or £100 a week - and that suits them fine. However, for the more ambitious Networker there is the opportunity to become very successful.

9. Word of mouth advertising

Networking works through people getting out into the world and referring companies rely on their participants to get out there and refer their products to other people. You have been doing this for years and not getting paid for it. Take the example of a good book that you have read, you'll recommend it to maybe four or five people. The same as a good movie, show or nice restaurant. You recommend that product or service to friends. Networking companies do the same thing, except they reward you for recommending their product. The primary reason why Network Marketing companies can pass so much money back to their distributors is the very fact that they do not spend millions of pounds on advertising and distribution. The distributors fulfil the role of promoting the product (via word of mouth advertising, i.e., recommending the products to friends, relatives and others in their sphere of influence. This includes their warm market and others whom they come into contact with on a day-to-day basis), and they also take on the roles of distributing those products. The money otherwise allocated to these two costly overhead items is what is used to pay the distributors. The commission that distributors receive is commonly referred to as a "word of mouth advertising bonus."

10. What do big corporations, governments, the military and religious organisations have in common?

The one thing that the Vatican, Pentagon, White House and large corporations all have in common is the type of structure that would appear to have a figurehead at the top, who work closely with maybe five or six key people, and below that, each one of those key people work with five or six key people of their own. It has been said that Jesus was the best Networker of all time. He had a front line of only twelve, but they spread the word, and still are spreading the word of Christianity to millions.

11. Why is network marketing so powerful?

Network marketing is so powerful because a number of things are accomplished so very simply and at the same time effectively.

I. Recruiting

In a conventional Direct Sales force the sales manager has to recruit his team. He then has to go about training them and also motivating them. This is usually highly inefficient and ineffective and usually the sales manager ends up spreading himself too thin. In MLM everyone has the chance to recruit new members or participants.

II. Training

Again in direct selling the sales manager has to train his team. There is only so much he can do and at the end of the day even if he trains them all brilliantly, unfortunately that's where the dissemination of knowledge ends. In networking you are responsible for training the people in your downline. This is one of the major reasons why you can earn so much money for training and motivating the people below you.

III. Cost Effective Marketing

Because everyone in the network has a chance to earn substantial income for effective work at little or no risk, the whole team is motivated to achieve, sell and recruit.

IV. Exponential or Geometric Growth

This one factor alone is responsible for making people millions and it's how you can make a fortune too. Because you "recruit two" who "recruit two" each, taking advantage of exponential growth, a substantial network builds very quickly, and you have a chance to earn on the products sold by people in your group a lot of money, especially if you have trained and motivated them well.

12. A Business of your Own, but not on Your Own

When you get involved in a Network Marketing company you are building your own business. Treat it like your own business and treat it as a big business, for that is exactly what it is. The good thing about networking is that there is always plenty of help and training available from others who wish you to succeed.

13. Rules, Regulations and Fair Trading

There are many laws and guidelines to protect consumers who wish to reap the rewards of Network Marketing. These laws include, but are not limited to, Trading Schemes Regulations 1997, Trading Schemes Act 1996, Prices Act 1974, Sale of Goods Act 1979, Fair Trading Act 1973. In the UK, the industry trade association for Network Marketing companies is the Direct Selling Association (DSA). This body has its own Codes and monitors its member Network Marketing companies to ensure they stick to both the law and the Codes. The DSA also runs a membership scheme so that legitimate companies can show that they are approved. Membership is not automatic, it is something for a new company to strive for. When achieved, members must display the DSA logo on all their paperwork, contracts etc.

14. How to tell a genuine opportunity from a fake one

One of the real keys to looking out for a genuine opportunity is that it will have products and services that can be sold week after week without any problem. Beware of an opportunity that requires you to persuade others to join if you cannot see tangible proof of what the money is for.

The criteria which identify a respectable network marketing company are easy to identify.

1. Is there a genuine product or service?

2. Are there genuine customers, not just participants finding new participants on a "money-go-round"?

3. Is the pricing and commission structure fixed and published?

4. Are the Direct Selling Association's Rules being followed, even if the company is not a formal member of the DSA?

5. Is the company a member of the DSA, or is membership a realistic possibility? (Remember this is not automatic. Perfectly legitimate NM businesses are working towards DSA membership. Not being a member does not

necessarily indicate any flaw in the company.)

15. What next?

For those who wish to study the detail of the law, Appendices 1-3 provide a comprehensive overview of the subject and include five sections from Solicitors, Lawrence Graham, which are, of course, reproduced with their kind permission.

16. Appendix 1

The Trading Schemes Act 1996.

The main intention of the Trading Schemes Act is to prohibit schemes which offer substantial rewards to members for doing no more than recruiting others. To catch as many businesses in the definition as possible, there are now just two criteria to fulfil:

1) The participants in the scheme expect to receive financial benefits from any or all of the following:

- ✓ Introducing others to the scheme
- ✓ Promoting others within the scheme
- ✓ Supplying goods or services to any person
- ✓ The acquisition of goods or services by any person

2) Goods or Services or both provided by the person promoting the scheme are either:

- ✓ To be supplied by the participants (whether as participant for the promoter or otherwise) to other persons; or
- ✓ To be supplied by the promoter to persons introduced by participants.

Clearly, this covers all genuine Network Marketing organisations. Once again the importance of the supply of goods and/or services is emphasised and is evident in both sections of the new definition. It bears repeating that this is usually the best indicator of a legitimate operation. However, the new definition is much more satisfactory than the old one. The Scam Operations should easily fall under the rules and can then be prosecuted if they do not comply with them. Pyramids fall under the rules. (Chain letters were excluded from the regulations because the DTI already regarded them as illegal under the Lotteries Act).

17. Appendix 2

The Trading schemes Regulations 1997.

The Regulations contain detailed explanations as to how a legitimate Network Marketing business must be run. Some of the most important points are included below.

1. In the first 7 days of participation a new participant must not pay or agree to pay more than £200 to the company.

2. In the first 14 days of participation a new participant is entitled to all of their money back and they may return any goods they have bought without paying any handling charges for doing so.

3. A participant has buy-back rights which can be exercised on leaving the scheme.
4. The content of advertisements for the scheme is controlled. They must include the following warning:

Statutory Information:

a) It is illegal for a promoter or a participant in a trading scheme to persuade anyone to make a payment by promising benefits from others to join a trading scheme

b) Do not be misled by claims that high earnings are easily achieved. The content of contracts for the scheme is controlled. In addition to the above they must include the following:

c) If you sign this contract you have 14 days in which to cancel and get your money back.

Other matters covered by the regulations include:

- Pre-performance by the promoter
- Securities and guarantees
- Record keeping
- Recovery of commission on termination
- Civil consequences of contravention of the Regulations.

18.   Appendix 3

What the professionals look for.

The following 5 sections are reproduced by kind permission of our Solicitors -Lawrence Graham.

Pyramid scheme not defined in legislation.

1. The Fair Trading Act defines a "trading scheme" and then regulates (primarily through the Trading Schemes Regulations 1997) how those schemes should operate. However, a scheme which breaches a provision in the Trading Schemes Regulations is not necessarily an unlawful scheme or a pyramid scheme simply because of that breach. Conversely, a scheme may comply with the Trading Schemes

Regulations yet still be declared unlawful by the Courts. Although a "pyramid scheme" is not defined in the legislation, the type of scheme at which the Fair Trading Act is aimed was summarised in the Official Report of the House of Commons, namely: "Get-rich-quick schemes operating on the same basis as chain letters with each member recruiting further members. Members pay-out large sums in the expectation of a high return. These payments are nearly always based on unrealistic forecasts of earnings from recruitment. These forecasts are derived from the principle of geometric progression, leading to theoretical levels of recruitment reward which, in reality, are impossible to achieve."

Unlawful schemes, lotteries or against the public interest.

2. There is a difficulty in categorically stating that any particular scheme is lawful based on a review of its scheme documentation alone, as it is quite possible for the documentation used for a scheme to comply with all of the relevant regulations yet for the scheme itself to be unlawful. The main reason for this is that whilst the laws governing the scheme documents are relatively clear and can usually be complied with simply by "desk top" drafting (provided that the promoter then complies in practice with the terms of its own documents), the Fair Trading Act does not define categories of lawful or unlawful schemes; rather, it creates a couple of important specific offences and then regulates

schemes which fall within its definition of a "trading scheme". It is then left to the Courts to determine whether a particular trading scheme is unlawful, relying in the main either upon the scheme being against the "public interest", which may be because it is "inherently objectionable as being ultimately bound to fail", or because it is a "lottery", in addition to the specific "recruitment payments" offence under Section 120 (3) of the Fair Trading Act.

Money circulation schemes, chain letters and unlawful lotteries.

3. In the past schemes have been declared unlawful, for example, because they have no goods or services (such as the obvious "money circulation" or "chain

letter" schemes), or because although it has goods and services the rewards which participant in truth will receive are derived from orders placed by other participants and not from sales to end-users achieved by that participant. The Courts treat the latter such schemes as "lotteries" within the meaning of the Lotteries Act 1976, on the basis that because the rewards to be obtained by a participant result from orders given by persons over whom that participant has no control then such rewards depend, so far as he is concerned, not upon his skill or work but upon pure chance, and hence the scheme is a "lottery".

Why the participant is described as having no control over the orders placed.

4. Because the goods are not "genuine" goods which the participant has the ability to sell on their own merits he must rely upon other persons placing orders because they are motivated by a desire to participate in the scheme. In such cases the goods have been described as "a peg on which the lottery is hung" (Global Pioneers case1984).

So, for example, in the leading case of D.P.P. v Phillips (1934) the promoter bought a supply of notecases at less than 10 pence each and signed up distributors who had to buy a notecase for £1 and obtain orders for notecases from customers also for £1. The distributor earned no commission on the first three sales but thereafter qualified for a commission of 50 pence on each £1 notecase sold by the promoter on orders obtained by the distributor or his downline. The Court held that the scheme was an unlawful lottery as - with the exception of commission resulting from orders directly obtained by the distributor himself - all the commissions which he received were from orders given by persons over whom he had no control and would depend, so far as he was concerned, not upon his skill or work but upon pure chance. In the Phillips case Lord Hewart said "The Court has to disengage, if it can, the reality of the transaction from the appearance which for obvious reasons it is made to assume. In my opinion this was not a commercial transaction. The object of the seller and the object of the buyer were not concerned with notecases. They were concerned with the chance which the buyer might procure of obtaining a large sum of money by the operation of persons over whom he had no more control than he has over the countless laughter of the sea, which does not laugh when the sun is not shining. "Similarly, in the " Titan Business Club" (July 1996) the Court held that the scheme(which in its original form at the time of this Court Judgement involved no products or services but consisted entirely of the sale of participations in itself, with distributors receiving commissions from the membership fees paid by new members introduced by them") was an unlawful lottery. The Court approved the Phillips decision: Lord Justice Saville said "an over-analytical approach should not be adopted, but rather one of common sense. In the present case, the reality of the matter is undoubtedly that those persuaded to join the scheme did so and paid their money in the hope of the rewards that would result from those afterwards joining their particular "family tree".

"Misleading advertisements.

5. The Control of Misleading Advertisements Regulations 1988 give powers to the Office of Fair Trading to apply to Court for an injunction against any person appearing to be concerned with the publication of a misleading advertisement, and the Office of Fair Trading is most likely to take such action when a publisher has failed to respond to a complaint or finding by the ASA that the advertisement is in breach of its Codes. The essential concern of the Advertising Code is with the content of advertisements, applying the general principle that advertisements should be "legal,

decent, honest and truthful". It does not presume to judge whether what is being advertised is worth buying, nor does it act as censor on matters of taste.

The current situation

The 1973 Act allows the Secretary of State to create regulations governing the industry. The Act has recently been amended and what follows is a brief resume of the current position. Due to the difficulties experienced with the 1973 four part definition of a trading scheme, it was decided to broaden the new definition in order to catch as many schemes as possible, then create new regulations to control them. What is now the Trading Schemes Act 1996 was originally introduced to Parliament as a private members" bill by Sir Nicholas Scott with the support of the Direct Selling

Association (DSA) which is the industry watchdog. The Trading Schemes Act 1996 was passed and it was hoped that this would create workable system of regulation for the legitimate businesses, while expunging the current fraudsters and dissuading any prospective ones from starting up. The Direct selling industry was then worth about £1bn in retail trade and the Government recognised that it provided many people with an excellent opportunity for part time earnings. The Trading Schemes Act 1996 replaced Section 118 of The Fair Trading Act 1973with a two part definition for trading schemes. This was much wider than the previous definition and its purpose was to catch all versions of Network Marketing types of business. New regulations were then issued to make the businesses which now come under the Act comply with strict but fair criteria. This was to ensure that the public are protected, the scams are out of business and probably most important, the legitimate Network Marketing businesses can show that they are reputable and safe for the public to invest both their time and money in. The new regulations are called The Trading Schemes Regulations 1997. They became law on 6th February 1997. They replaced the old "Pyramid Selling Regulations 1989"

Personal Invitation from Ron G Holland to a Global Business Opportunity

Dear reader,

After 40 years of creating businesses and taking existing businesses to the next level, including big network marketing companies, I have come across a very special business opportunity to which I would like to invite you personally. I would love you to join my team and take advantage of this lucrative global SILVER AND GOLD COINS BUSINESS that literally anyone can do. This is the lowest risk and the lowest outlay business opportunity I have seen in years, and it's actually something that works for everyone.

Simply follow the link and leave your details, and I will personally contact you very quickly to show you how you can build and protect your wealth while helping others do the same. Type the link below into your web browser:

www.ISNCoins.com/RonAtWealth

Onwards and Upwards

Ron G Holland

Take action!

www.ingramcontent.com/pod-product-compliance
Lightning Source LLC
Chambersburg PA
CBHW070431180526
45158CB00017B/976